KAIROS PALESTINE
a moment of truth

I0171215

INTRODUCTION

Kairos Palestine is the Christian Palestinian's word to the world about what is happening in Palestine. Its importance stems from the sincere expression of Palestinian Christian concerns for their people and their view of the moment of history they are living through. It is deeply committed to Jesus' way of love and nonviolence even in the face of entrenched injustice. It seeks to be prophetic in addressing things as they are, without equivocation. It is a contemporary, ecumenical confession of faith and call to action. Its tone and its theology echo similar Christian manifestos written in times of crisis, e.g., at the rise of Nazism (*Barmen Declaration*, 1934), during the Civil Rights Movement in the U.S.A. (*Letter from the Birmingham Jail*, 1963), and amidst the struggle to end Apartheid in South Africa (*Kairos Document*, 1985). This appeal was drafted and endorsed by a broad coalition of Palestinian Christian leaders–Catholic, Orthodox, mainline Protestant and evangelical.

SECTION 1
What is the *Kairos Palestine* document and why should we study it?

What is *Kairos*?

> *Kairos* is the Greek word for that special time of opportunity when we are invited to confess our faith by joining in God's redemptive activity. The Palestinian Christian authors of this document have declared "a moment of truth" when "a word of faith and hope" must be spoken "from the heart of Palestinian suffering" and heard by the world Church.

Why study *Kairos Palestine*?

Mennonites have been building relationships in Palestine-Israel for more than 65 years. An important expression of this work has been and continues to be education and advocacy, drawing attention to the suffering in Palestine and communicating the stories of Palestinian and Israeli peacebuilders to U.S. audiences. This includes lifting up the voices of Palestinian Christians and responding to their call for advocacy.

The Executive Director of Mennonite Church USA, writing on behalf of the Executive Board in 2011, encouraged "members of Mennonite Church USA in various settings to read and discuss this document [*Kairos Palestine*]... and to consider how you might be part of this response. Specifically we invite you to take steps to: learn about the situation in Israel/Palestine, including visiting the region and meeting with Christian brothers and sisters there; re-examine what the Bible says about the land of Israel and engage in conversation with each other about the theology of Christian Zionism and its impact on Christian brothers and sisters in the region; consider how our financial lives are enmeshed in the policies of occupation, especially through our tax dollars and investments; deepen our commitment to the way of the cross, which binds together great love for every person and courageous resistance to injustice and sin."

The 2015 Delegate Assembly of Mennonite Church USA, after earlier tabling a resolution on Israel-Palestine, unanimously passed a follow-up resolution titled "A Statement of Support for Our Palestinian and Israeli Partners in Peacemaking." The resolution commits the church to "strive to understand more fully the social, economic and political context in which you live, work and pray; to reflect on our own theological and political understandings of the land of Israel-Palestine; and to discern ways we can seek a more just future for all peoples of Israel and Palestine."

What is the purpose of this lesson plan?

To best hear and understand the voices of Christian Palestinians we need a common understanding of some of the political and religious issues that are a consequence of the creation of the state of Israel and Israel's subsequent annexation of East Jerusalem and military occupation of the West Bank and Gaza. Given the polarized and often biased media portrayal of issues involving Israel and Palestine, it is sometimes difficult for Americans to have thoughtful and respectful discussions of these issues. The purpose of this lesson plan is to facilitate a meaningful discussion of *Kairos Palestine* by providing the context for their plea, to define terms or facts on the ground referred to in the document, and to frame issues for discussion.

Who prepared this lesson plan?

Following the passage of "A Statement of Support for Our Palestinian and Israeli Partners in Peacemaking" by the 2015 Delegate Assembly of Mennonite

Church USA, the Rev. Alex Awad, former Dean of Bethlehem Bible College, urged delegates to make "a serious study of the *Kairos Document*." The Mennonite Palestine-Israel Network (MennoPIN) received permission from the Israel Palestine Mission Network (IPMN) of the Presbyterian Church (U.S.A.) to adapt their previously-published study guide for use in Mennonite congregations.

To whom is *Kairos Palestine* addressed?

Local Christians, Palestinian and Israeli religious and political leaders and civil societies, the international community, all Christians and all Churches around the world.

What is the central message of *Kairos Palestine*?

In the midst of "the absence of hope," Christian Palestinians proclaim a word of faith, hope, and love. At the same time they make the following declarations:

- The decades-old Israeli military occupation of Palestinian territories is a sin against God and humanity.

- Any theology or interpretation of the Bible by Christians or Jews that justifies this occupation is "far from Christian teachings."[1]

- Christians are called to confront evil and injustice, with a creative, courageous, nonviolent resistance which "[sees] the image of God in the face of the enemy" and has "love as its logic." A resistance based on love of enemy and a repudiation of revenge is the only hope for a just peace and reconciliation.

- *Kairos Palestine* affirms particular boycotts, divestment and sanctions as an expression of nonviolent resistance to injustice and as tools for justice, peace and security for all.

What *Kairos Palestine* is not.

Kairos Palestine is not a comprehensive analysis of the Middle East or of the complex history of the Israeli/Palestinian conflict. Instead, it portrays the reality on the ground today in the West Bank and Gaza and the Palestinian Christian response to the injustices suffered by the Palestinian people living under military occupation.

Is *Kairos Palestine* balanced?

Kairos Palestine is the authentic voice of Palestinian Christians and is their description of what is happening today in their land and to their

---

1 The use of the phrase "is far from Christian teachings" in the Kairos document (see 2.5 and page 27 under "Message from the Authors'") appears to carry the same force as a charge of heresy.

people. This narrative was not intended to include other perspectives. Rather, it seeks to address the many forms of imbalance now present in many international conversations about Palestine and Israel, including 1) the misuse of the Bible and theology to support injustice, 2) the double standards used by the international community that contribute to Palestinian suffering, and 3) the profound imbalance of power between Israelis and Palestinians in the media, at the negotiation table, and on the ground. The authors of *Kairos* cry out against this lethal imbalance by declaring the truth as they understand it, and confessing their faith in the Gospel of Jesus Christ, which they believe has the power to bring an end to hatred and violence and transform enemies into friends.

SECTION 2
The Reality on the Ground – Background Facts and Maps

Kairos Palestine presumes that readers are familiar with some of the basic facts regarding Israel's occupation of the West Bank and Gaza: illegal Israeli settlements, the separation wall, checkpoints, and the deprivation of human rights and freedom suffered by the Palestinians. Because U.S. media rarely provide all of these facts, below is a brief summary of the existing situation on the ground that may assist the reader of the *Kairos Palestine* document.

Palestinian Land Expropriation 1948-1967

Under the 1947 U.N. partition resolution, 56% of the land area of Palestine was designated for a Jewish state and 44% for an Arab state. However, in the war that followed Israel's declaration of independence in 1948, Israel occupied 78% of the land, leaving only 22% of Palestine for an eventual Arab state (see map "Palestine loss of land 1946-2000," page 5). 750,000 Palestinians fled for safety or were forcibly removed from their property and prohibited from returning to their land. Instead, Israel expropriated their land in violation of U.N. resolutions.

The *Nakba*

The 1948 expulsion of 750,000 Palestinians from what became the state of Israel is known by Palestinians as the *Nakba*, meaning the "disaster," "catastrophe," or "cataclysm." More than 60 percent of the 1.4 million Palestinians living in what now is Israel, as well as 750,000 Palestinians in the West Bank and 1.2 million Palestinians in Gaza, are "internal refugees," having been displaced from their original land and homes. More than 530 Palestinian villages were depopulated and completely destroyed to erase their memory. Today more than 7 million Palestinian refugees are still displaced and dispossessed.

4

Palestinian loss of land, 1946 to 2010

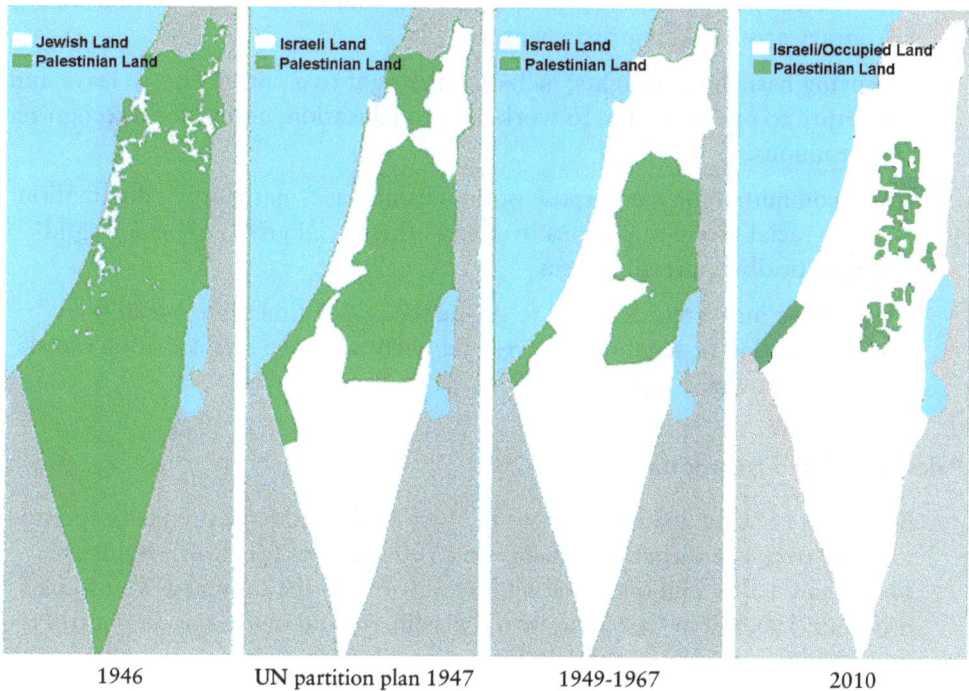

| Jewish Land Palestinian Land | Israeli Land Palestinian Land | Israeli Land Palestinian Land | Israeli/Occupied Land Palestinian Land |

| 1946 | UN partition plan 1947 | 1949-1967 | 2010 |

Palestine-Israel Action Group, Ann Arbor Friends Meeting | piag_@mac.com

Israel's Occupation of the West Bank and Gaza

The internationally recognized boundary of Israel, which was established by the Armistice of 1949, is shown in the third panel of the maps, above. Palestinians living in the West Bank, including East Jerusalem, lived under Jordanian rule, and Palestinians living in Gaza lived under Egyptian rule, pending the establishment of a Palestinian state that would control these areas. In 1967, after a war with Jordan and Egypt, Israeli military forces occupied the West Bank and Gaza. Under international law these territories are considered to be militarily occupied by Israel and not part of Israel. They are "occupied Palestine" and are administered by the Israeli military under military law, not by Israeli civilian authorities.

International Law Regarding Populations Under Military Occupation

International laws define the basic human rights of people under military occupation and what constitutes crimes against humanity. International law prohibits:

- The expropriation of landed property belonging to a racial group or groups or to members thereof.

- Refusing land owners the right to return to their property after a military conflict.

- Denying basic human freedoms, including the freedom of movement, residence, opinion, expression, and peaceful assembly, and freedom from arbitrary arrest and imprisonment.

- Denying basic human rights, including the right to a nationality, to leave and to return to one's country, to work, and to education, and to form recognized trade unions.

- Acts committed for the purpose of establishing and maintaining domination by one racial group of persons over any other racial group of persons and systematically oppressing them.

- Legislative measures, designed to divide the population along racial lines by the creation of separate reserves and ghettos for the members of a racial group or groups.

Palestinian Land Expropriation 1967-2015

Between 1967 and 2015, vast areas of West Bank land have been expropriated to allow over 121 illegal settlements and 100 outposts for Jewish residents. More than half a million Israeli settlers now live in the occupied West Bank, including 190,000 in East Jerusalem. Palestinian land ownership or control is now confined to 13% of pre-1947 Palestine (shown on the fourth panel of the map, page 5). Since 2007 Gaza has been subjected to a full Israeli blockade.

The Centrality of Jerusalem

Shortly after the war of 1967, Israel unilaterally annexed East Jerusalem and surrounding Palestinian lands in defiance of international law and in spite of vigorous condemnation by the international community. Yet "Jerusalem is the heart of our reality," declares *Kairos* (1.1.8) and is "the first issue that should be negotiated" (9.5). Because Jerusalem holds such deep religious and cultural significance for Jews, Muslims, and Christians, and because Jerusalem is also the heart of the Palestinian economy, a shared Jerusalem lies at the heart of any solution to the conflict, be it a two-state or a one-state solution. The continuing expulsion of Palestinians from their homes in East Jerusalem, the increasing settlement of Israeli Jews in East Jerusalem, and the repetitive Israeli claim that all of Jerusalem is now and will always be a part of Israel, are major obstacles to peace.

Restrictions on Palestinian Freedom of Residence

The Israeli military command in the occupied West Bank has approved almost no building permits for Palestinians living in the rural undeveloped land. However, building permits for settlement colonies with half a million Jewish residents have been approved on Palestinian land in violation of international law. Between 1967 and 2001, almost no Palestinians were given permits for housing construction in East Jerusalem. However, 46,978 housing units have been built for Jewish settlers in East Jerusalem. From June 1967 to June

2009, over 24,000 Palestinian homes have been demolished in the occupied territories.

Restrictions on Palestinian Freedom of Movement

Hundreds of checkpoints and roadblocks in the occupied West Bank restrict Palestinians' freedom of movement to their homes, businesses, schools, jobs, hospitals, and farms. Palestinians are dehumanized and routinely suffer indeterminate waiting, humiliating treatment, uncertainty, and denial of access at checkpoints.

Segregated roads: Segregated roads, which Israel calls "bypass roads," link settlement colonies with one another and with Israel (see map, below). The 493 miles of bypass roads provide unrestricted access to Israeli vehicles but restrict or prohibit Palestinian travel. These roads cut off Palestinians from their agricultural land, schools, hospitals, markets, and extended families and carve up the West Bank into isolated enclaves.

Separation Wall: In 2002 the Israeli government began building a "separation wall" in the West Bank. Much of the Separation Wall is constructed between Palestinian homes and their farmland, businesses, schools, hospitals, and the homes of family and friends. In East Jerusalem the Separation Wall is constructed through the middle of a once contiguous city, much like the Berlin Wall. With 85% of the wall constructed inside the West Bank and not on the internationally-recognized Green Line, the wall's main purpose is not security, but rather to separate Palestinians from Israeli settlement colonies on expropriated Palestinian land.

Israel has divided the population along racial lines: The settlement colonies, the segregated roads that connect them, and the Separation Wall restrict Palestinians to isolated reserves or ghettos, devastate the Palestinian

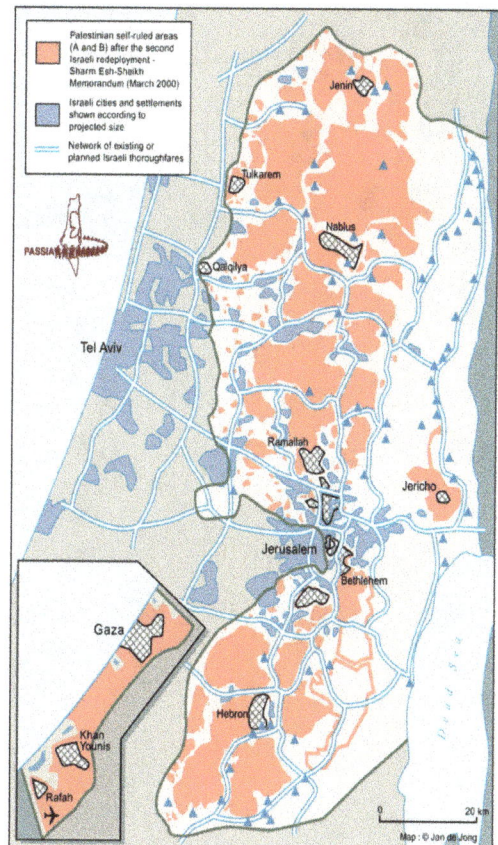

Segregation roads that link settlement colonies in the West Bank with Israel allow unrestricted settler movement but allow limited or no access to Palestinians.

Palestinian Academic Society for the Study of International Affairs (PASSIA) www.passia.org

economy, and prevent the creation of a viable, contiguous, sovereign, and independent Palestinian state. Rather than decrease, the number of settlements and segregated roads increased during the 1993 Oslo peace negotiations.

The West Bank reserves or ghettos to which Palestinians are confined are shown in the map, below. Palestinians are denied access to the white areas on the map.

Foundation for Middle East Peace www.fmep.org

Palestinian Academic Society for the Study of International Affairs (PASSIA) www.passia.org

The Separation Wall (blue line) is not on the internationally recognized boundary between Israel and Palestine. Large swaths of Palestinian territory are on the "Israel side" of the Wall.

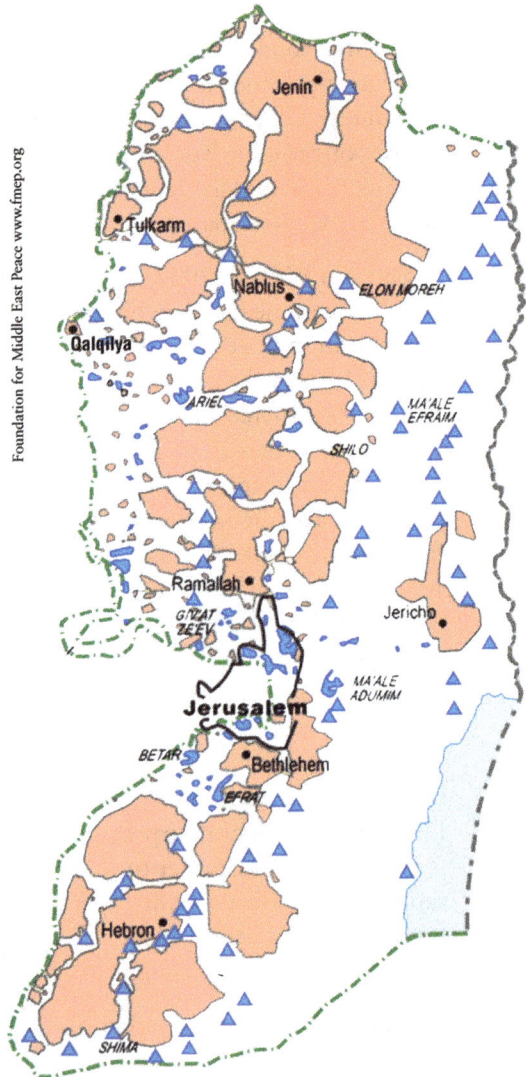

Reserves or ghettos (shown in pink) confine Palestinians into 64 isolated and totally surrounded canton-like reserves in the West Bank. The triangles are major Israeli settlement colonies.

The One-State and Two-State Options for Israel and Palestine

Right now, there is a *de facto* one-state solution in Israel, with Israel controlling the land and resources and unequal rights for Palestinians and Israelis. Alternatively, a one-state solution could mean that all the residents of Israel-Palestine live in one country with equal rights and share all the land. The two-state solution is for Israel and Palestine to be two different states, each being contiguous, economically viable, and independent. Many today fear that a one-state solution with equal rights for all is not viable because Israel believes there must be a majority of Jews in any Israeli state and that the demographics of one state would end in a Palestinian majority. At the same time, many fear that the two-state solution is no longer viable because Israeli settlements with more than a half-million people in Palestine are precluding a contiguous, economically viable, independent state.

SECTION 3

A Four-Week Lesson Plan for Congregational Study

Message to the class leader:

This lesson plan is organized around three major sections of *Kairos Palestine*: Week One, Faith, Hope, and Love (sections 2, 3, 4 and 10); Week Two, the effects on Palestinians of Israeli military occupation (section 1); and Week Three, the call to action addressed to various groups (sections 5-9). Week Four opens conversation about specific actions and invites prayers for peace. You will need the following materials to lead this study: a Bible; a copy of *Kairos Palestine: Four-Week Congregational Study Plan* for each class member.

In Week 2, it is suggested that the class view part of Chapter 2 ("The Big Picture") from the Steadfast Hope DVD (11 minutes). *Steadfast Hope: The Palestinian Quest for Just Peace* is a curriculum produced by the Presbyterian Israel Palestine Mission Network (IPMN) that includes a 48-page booklet and an 80-minute DVD. (Available singly or with volume discount at http://store.pcusa.org or 1-800-524-2612. Ask for item #26466-09-001. The video is also available via the IPMN website www.israelpalestinemissionnetwork.org/main/component/content/article/5/3-steadfast-hope.

In Week 4, it is suggested that the class view the video "Children of the Nakba" produced by Mennonite Central Committee. (Available via the MennoPIN Resource Page at www.mennopin.org/congregational-resources).

Additional resources include *What is Palestine-Israel? Answers to Common Questions,* by Sonia Weaver (commissioned by Mennonite Central Committee, available through Mennonite Media); *Under Vine and Fig Tree: Biblical Theologies of Land and the Palestinian-Israeli Conflict,* ed. by Alain Epp Weaver (available from Cascadia); and the MCC-produced video "Dividing Wall." (Available via the MennoPIN Resource Page at www.mennopin.org/congregational-resources).

A Word of Faith, Hope, and Love

1. Welcome and opening prayer (5 minutes)

2. If copies of the *Kairos Palestine: Four-Week Congregational Study Plan* have not been distributed ahead of time, pass them out at the beginning of class.

3. The leader presents an overview of the study and of *Kairos Palestine*. (5 minutes)

4. Divide the class into three groups. Ask one group to read and discuss section 2 on Faith; another group to read and discuss section 3 on Hope; and the last group to read and discuss section 4 on Love. (15 minutes)

5. Ask one person from each group to answer the question: What surprised you or caught your group's attention in the section you discussed? (10 minutes)

6. General class discussion, using questions that arise from the group or some of the following questions. (15 minutes)

   • Is this the usual way we understand the meaning of faith, hope, and love?

   • How might some biblical interpretations transform the living Word into a "dead letter" that is "used as a weapon...to deprive us of our rights in our own land" (2.2.2; 2.3.3)? How might some Churches "offer a theological cover-up" for injustice? (6.1)

   • How does the Palestinian Christian commitment to active nonviolence in a situation of significant injustice challenge Mennonite commitments to peacemaking?

   • *Kairos Palestine* has been called "A letter from a Palestinian Jail." What similarities and differences do you find between the current Palestinian struggle and the Civil Rights struggle in the U.S. during the 1950s and 1960s? Do you find any echoes of the writings of Martin Luther King, Jr?

7. Wrap up and share the assignment for next week which is to read section 1 of *Kairos Palestine* and pages 1-5 and 8-9 of this lesson plan. Closing prayer. (5 minutes)

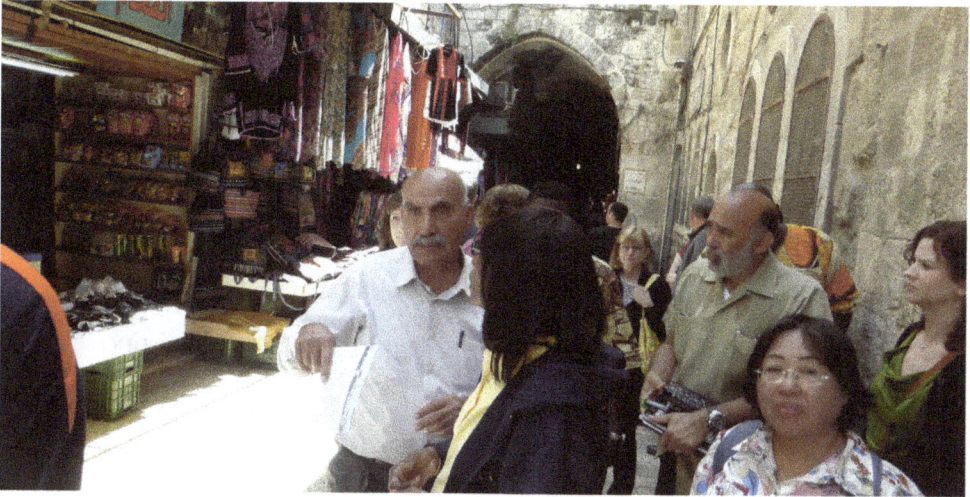

Photo: Mark Schildt

"Come and See" tours were initiated by the MCUSA Executive Board, which hopes to send 100 Mennonite Church leaders to Israel/Palestine over five years. Here, participants in an April, 2015 tour are on a political tour of the Old City of Jerusalem.

② WEEK 2
The Reality on the Ground

1. Welcome and opening prayer (5 minutes)

2. Leader asks each participant, "Please turn to the person next to you and discuss your initial reactions to the assigned reading for today about the Reality on the Ground." (5 minutes)

3. Class discussion of the Reality on the Ground, using questions that arise from the group or some of the following: (30 minutes)

   • How much did you know about the Israeli military occupation of the Palestinian territories before reading *Kairos Palestine*?

   • How do the various laws, policies, and practices of the Israeli military occupation contribute to turning "our towns and villages into prisons"? (1.1.1)

   • How do you respond to the comparison of the "de facto" state theology of the occupation with the South African state theology of Apartheid. What name would you give to this "de facto" state theology?

   • Show the first 11 minutes of Chapter 2 ("The Big Picture") of the Steadfast Hope DVD (also available via the IPMN website at www.israelpalestinemissionnetwork.org/main/component/content/article/5/3-steadfast-hope).

   • Wrap-up and share the assignment for next week (read sections 5-10 of *Kairos Palestine*) and offer a closing prayer. (5 minutes)

3 WEEK THREE
What Does the Lord Require of Us?

1. Welcome and opening prayer (5 minutes)

2. Ask the group to list on the board questions and issues that remain from the last two weeks. (10 minutes)

3. General discussion of the following: (35 minutes)

   • *Kairos Palestine* is addressed to several different groups. What distinct messages are addressed to each specific audience? Can you identify any parts of the text addressed to Fatah and Hamas (the two major Palestinian political parties), to Israel, and to the U.S.A.? What is the message to the global Christian church?

   • Why does *Kairos Palestine* accuse the international community of using "double standards" for Palestine and Israel? (Section 7)

   • Section 4.2.6 supports an economic and commercial boycott of everything produced by the occupation. Section 7 calls for "the beginning of a system of economic sanctions and boycott to be applied against Israel." In 2013, the Mennonite Central Committee US Board decided not to invest in companies that benefit from violence against Palestinians, Israelis or others. How do you respond to the use of economic measures as a form of non-violent resistance?

   • Which sections of *Kairos Palestine* may resonate with or disturb members of your congregation?

   • Some American Jews have attacked *Kairos Palestine*, saying it delegitimizes the state of Israel and declares that Christianity replaces God's covenant with the Jews. Did you find any evidence of this in your reading of *Kairos Palestine*? Does *Kairos Palestine* question the validity of God's covenant with the Jews?

Mennonite Central Committee | Ryan Rodrick Beiler

Mennonite Central Committee worker Sarah Thompson joined volunteers organized by Omar Haramy of MCC partner organization Sabeel to plant olive trees at the farm of the Nassar family in Nahalin, Palestine, in 2011. The Nassars are Palestinian Christians whose land was threatened with confiscation by nearby Israeli settlements.

4. Wrap up and closing prayer (5 minutes)

4 WEEK 4
Act for Peace, Pray for Peace

1. Welcome and Opening Prayer (5 minutes)

2. View "Children of the Nakba" (produced by Mennonite Central Committee, available at www.mennopin.org/congregational-resources) (25 minutes)

3. General discussion: (15 minutes)

   • How can you, your congregation, and your conference respond to this confession and call to action from our Christian brothers and sisters in the land of our Savior's birth?

   • What do you personally feel called to do or share given this knowledge?

   • Who do you know that would benefit from this study, or further study of the *Steadfast Hope* curriculum?

4. Prayers for peace (10 minutes)

   • Pray for just peace for all of the people of Israel and Palestine;

   • Pray for wisdom for the leaders of nations;

   • Pray for strength and courage for all peace-makers;

5. Closing

In April 2015, a West Coast "Come and See" tour organized the MCUSA visited the Lajee Center in Bethlehem.

Photo: Mark Schildt

Brief history of Mennonite involvement in Palestine-Israel

Mennonites have been building relationships in Palestine-Israel for over 60 years, working alongside Palestinians and Israelis for peace with justice. After the horrors of the Holocaust, many Jews welcomed the creation of the State of Israel, viewing it as a potential safe haven. The establishment of Israel in 1948, however, went hand in hand with the massive dispossession and displacement of over 750,000 Palestinians and the destruction of over 500 Palestinian towns and villages.

Mennonite Central Committee (MCC) responded in 1949 to this newly created refugee crisis with material assistance and numerous other ways including education and rural development. Another example was selling needlework made by Palestinian refugee women, one of the first products sold by what eventually grew into the alternative trading organization Ten Thousand Villages.

Over the years MCC developed bonds of friendship with the Palestinian churches, joining them in their ministry, including partnerships with the Latin Patriarchate School in Zababdeh and the Bethlehem Bible College. Since Israel's occupation of East Jerusalem, the West Bank, and the Gaza Strip in 1967, MCC has supported the work of both Palestinians and Israelis committed to non-violence and a future of peace, justice, and reconciliation for both peoples. The MCC Peace Section organized its first study tour to Palestine-Israel in 1969. MCC has continued to organize delegations, currently one each year from the United States and Canada, signaling the significant role of educating North American Mennonites. MCC has produced various periodicals, books, and education resources as well as placed hundreds of workers and volunteers in Palestine-Israel. In 2013, the MCC U.S. Board decided not to invest in companies that benefit from violence against Palestinians, Israelis or others.

Mennonite Mission Network (MMN, then Mennonite Board of Missions) has had a presence in Palestine-Israel since the mid-1950s in conjunction with **Eastern**

Photo courtesy of Al Najd Development Forum

Volunteers delivered mattresses to families who opened their homes to other Gazans displaced by the Israel-Hamas conflict in 2014. Mennonite Central Committee provided bedding and supplies that were distributed through partner organization Al Najd Development Forum.

Mennonite Missions (EMM, then Eastern Mennonite Board of Missions and Charities). This work was initially focused on working with the Messianic Jewish movement in Israel. MMN staff currently serve on the faculty of Israel College of the Bible. Since the mid-1960s this work has also included partnering with Palestinian Christian at Nazareth Hospital and schools, as well as helping to establish Nazareth Village, which has seen a steady flow of North American volunteers and visitors.

Christian Peacemaker Teams (CPT) has had a presence in Hebron, in the Occupied West Bank, since 1994. This presence has included school patrols that accompany children, monitoring settler violence and soldier home invasions, and working against home demolitions. CPT supports Palestinian-led nonviolent resistance to Israel's military occupation and educates people in North America. Education campaigns have included the "Campaign for Secure Dwellings" (1997-2000, in whose first year 58 churches were matched with Palestinian families), "Tent for Lent" campaign (March 1999), and "Urgent Action" international letter writing campaigns. CPT organizes several delegations to Palestine every year and endorsed the Boycott, Divestment, and Sanctions (BDS) campaign in 2010.

Mennonite educational institutions have exposed hundreds of Mennonite students to the situation in Palestine-Israel through course work and learning tours. **Eastern Mennonite University** (EMU) has had a Middle East Cross-Cultural semester for decades. Both **Bethel College** and Bluffton University run a delegation every other year. **Eastern Mennonite Seminary** also organizes regular learning tours. Mennonite college and university campuses have also been the site of student activism over the years. EMU students started a "Students for Morally Responsible Investment" group that organized a student gathering outside of the school's Board of Trustees meeting in November 2010. Goshen College students constructed a replica of Israel's separation wall on that campus in February 2011, and several students visited and volunteered in Palestine that summer.

In 2007, **Mennonite Church USA** (MCUSA) organized a delegation of denominational leaders from across its agencies to visit Palestine-Israel with the purpose of engaging the discussion on divestment. As a result, the delegation wrote an Open Letter "Becoming Peacemakers in Israel/Palestine." The Open Letter was presented at the MCUSA 2007 San Jose Convention. In 2011, the MCUSA Executive Board issued a response to *Kairos Palestine* with a letter to Palestinian Christians as well as a letter to members of Mennonite Church USA. The first "Come and See" trip, initiated by MCUSA Executive Board with funding from MMN, Everence, and MCC U.S., took place in 2014 with the goal of sending 100 Mennonite Church leaders on learning tours in five years.

In 2013, a **Mennonite Palestine Israel Network** (MennoPIN) was formed to support advocacy and action, develop and promote educational resources, and join with people of faith and conscience around the world who share a passion for peace with justice in Palestine-Israel. MennoPIN has given particular attention to the Kairos Palestine call and creating space for advocacy and action on the issue of boycott, divestment, and sanctions within Mennonite Church USA.

For more that sixty-five years, Mennonites have lived, studied and ministered in Palestine and Israel ... We open our hearts when we again hear of the suffering you experience in an occupied land as homes are taken from you, families and communities are separated by walls and checkpoints, and countless large and small indignities and humiliations are visited upon you each day.

—Excerpt from a 2011 letter written on behalf of the Mennonite Church USA Executive Board in response to *Kairos Palestine*

KAIROS PALESTINE | 2009

A moment of truth:
A word of faith, hope and love from the heart of Palestinian suffering

Introduction

We, a group of Christian Palestinians, after prayer, reflection and an exchange of opinion, cry out from within the suffering in our country, under the Israeli occupation, with a cry of hope in the absence of all hope, a cry full of prayer and faith in a God ever vigilant, in God's divine providence for all the inhabitants of this land. Inspired by the mystery of God's love for all, the mystery of God's divine presence in the history of all peoples and, in a particular way, in the history of our country, we proclaim our word based on our Christian faith and our sense of Palestinian belonging – a word of faith, hope and love.

Why now? Because today we have reached a dead end in the tragedy of the Palestinian people. The decision-makers content themselves with managing the crisis rather than committing themselves to the serious task of finding a way to resolve it. The hearts of the faithful are filled with pain and with questioning: What is the international community doing? What are the political leaders in Palestine, in Israel and in the Arab world doing? What is the Church doing? The problem is not just a political one. It is a policy in which human beings are destroyed, and this must be of concern to the Church.

We address ourselves to our brothers and sisters, members of our Churches in this land We call out as Christians and as Palestinians to our religious and political leaders, to our Palestinian society and to the Israeli society, to the international community, and to our Christian brothers and sisters in the Churches around the world .

1. The reality on the ground

1.1 *"They say: 'Peace, peace' when there is no peace"* (Jer. 6:14). These days, everyone is speaking about peace in the Middle East and the peace process. So far, however, these are simply words; the reality is one of Israeli occupation of Palestinian territories, deprivation of our freedom and all that results from this situation:

1.1.1 The separation wall erected on Palestinian territory, a large part of which has been confiscated for this purpose, has turned our towns and villages into prisons, separating them from one another, making them dispersed and divided cantons. Gaza, especially after the cruel war Israel launched against it during December 2008 and January 2009, continues to live in inhuman conditions, under permanent blockade and cut off from the other Palestinian territories .

1.1.2 Israeli settlements ravage our land in the name of God and in the name of force, controlling our natural resources, including water and agricultural land, thus depriving hundreds of thousands of Palestinians, and constituting an obstacle to any political solution.

1.1.3 Reality is the daily humiliation to which we are subjected at the military checkpoints, as we make our way to jobs, schools or hospitals.

1.1.4 Reality is the separation between members of the same family, making family life impossible for thousands of Palestinians, especially where one of the spouses does not have an Israeli identity card.

1.1.5 Religious liberty is severely restricted; the freedom of access to the holy places is denied under the pretext of security. Jerusalem and its holy places are out of bounds for many Christians and Muslims from the West Bank and the Gaza strip. Even Jerusalemites face restrictions during the religious feasts. Some of our Arab clergy are regularly barred from entering Jerusalem .

1.1.6 Refugees are also part of our reality. Most of them are still living in camps under difficult circumstances. They have been waiting for their right of return, generation after generation. What will be their fate?

1.1.7 And the prisoners? The thousands of prisoners languishing in Israeli prisons are part of our reality. The Israelis move heaven and earth to gain the release of one prisoner, and those thousands of Palestinian prisoners, when will they have their freedom?

1.1.8 Jerusalem is the heart of our reality. It is, at the same time, symbol of peace and sign of conflict. While the separation wall divides Palestinian neighbourhoods, Jerusalem continues to be emptied of its Palestinian citizens, Christians and Muslims. Their identity cards are confiscated, which means the loss of their right to reside in Jerusalem. Their homes are demolished or expropriated. Jerusalem, city of reconciliation, has become a city of discrimination and exclusion, a source of struggle rather than peace .

1.2 Also part of this reality is the Israeli disregard of international law and international resolutions, as well as the paralysis of the Arab world and the international community in the face of this contempt. Human rights are violated and despite the various reports of local and international human rights' organizations, the injustice continues.

1.2.1 Palestinians within the State of Israel, who have also suffered a historical injustice, although they are citizens and have the rights and obligations of citizenship, still suffer from discriminatory policies. They too are waiting to enjoy full rights and equality like all other citizens in the state.

1.3 Emigration is another element in our reality. The absence of any vision or spark of hope for peace and freedom pushes young people, both Muslim and Christian, to emigrate. Thus the land is deprived of its most important and richest resource –

educated youth. The shrinking number of Christians, particularly in Palestine, is one of the dangerous consequences, both of this conflict, and of the local and international paralysis and failure to find a comprehensive solution to the problem.

1.4 In the face of this reality, Israel justifies its actions as self-defence, including occupation, collective punishment and all other forms of reprisals against the Palestinians. In our opinion, this vision is a reversal of reality. Yes, there is Palestinian resistance to the occupation. However, if there were no occupation, there would be no resistance, no fear and no insecurity. This is our understanding of the situation. Therefore, we call on the Israelis to end the occupation. Then they will see a new world in which there is no fear, no threat but rather security, justice and peace.

1.5 The Palestinian response to this reality was diverse. Some responded through negotiations: that was the official position of the Palestinian Authority, but it did not advance the peace process. Some political parties followed the way of armed resistance. Israel used this as a pretext to accuse the Palestinians of being terrorists and was able to distort the real nature of the conflict, presenting it as an Israeli war against terror, rather than an Israeli occupation faced by Palestinian legal resistance aiming at ending it.

> 1.5.1 The tragedy worsened with the internal conflict among Palestinians themselves, and with the separation of Gaza from the rest of the Palestinian territory. It is noteworthy that, even though the division is among Palestinians themselves, the international community bears an important responsibility for it since it refused to deal positively with the will of the Palestinian people expressed in the outcome of democratic and legal elections in 2006.

Again, we repeat and proclaim that our Christian word in the midst of all this, in the midst of our catastrophe, is a word of faith, hope and love.

2. A word of faith

We believe in one God, a good and just God

2.1 We believe in God, one God, Creator of the universe and of humanity. We believe in a good and just God, who loves each one of his creatures. We believe that every human being is created in God's image and likeness and that every one's dignity is derived from the dignity of the Almighty One. We believe that this dignity is one and the same in each and all of us. This means for us, here and now, in this land in particular, that God created us not so that we might engage in strife and conflict but rather that we might come and know and love one another, and together build up the land in love and mutual respect.

> 2.1.1 We also believe in God's eternal Word, His only Son, our Lord Jesus Christ, whom God sent as the Saviour of the world.

> 2.1.2 We believe in the Holy Spirit, who accompanies the Church and all humanity on its journey. It is the Spirit that helps us to understand Holy Scripture, both Old and New Testaments, showing their unity, here and now. The Spirit makes manifest the revelation of God to humanity, past, present and future.

How do we understand the word of God?

2.2 We believe that God has spoken to humanity, here in our country: *"Long ago God spoke to our ancestors in many and various ways by the prophets, but in these last days God has spoken to us by a Son, whom God appointed heir of all things, through whom he also created the worlds"* (Heb. 1:1-2)

2.2.1 We, Christian Palestinians, believe, like all Christians throughout the world, that Jesus Christ came in order to fulfil the Law and the Prophets. He is the Alpha and the Omega, the beginning and the end, and in his light and with the guidance of the Holy Spirit, we read the Holy Scriptures. We meditate upon and interpret Scripture just as Jesus Christ did with the two disciples on their way to Emmaus. As it is written in the Gospel according to Saint Luke: *"Then beginning with Moses and all the prophets, he interpreted to them the things about himself in all the scriptures"* (Lk 24:27)

2.2.2 Our Lord Jesus Christ came, proclaiming that the Kingdom of God was near. He provoked a revolution in the life and faith of all humanity. He came with *"a new teaching"* (Mk 1:27), casting a new light on the Old Testament, on the themes that relate to our Christian faith and our daily lives, themes such as the promises, the election, the people of God and the land. We believe that the Word of God is a living Word, casting a particular light on each period of history, manifesting to Christian believers what God is saying to us here and now. For this reason, it is unacceptable to transform the Word of God into letters of stone that pervert the love of God and His providence in the life of both peoples and individuals. This is precisely the error in fundamentalist Biblical interpretation that brings us death and destruction when the word of God is petrified and transmitted from generation to generation as a dead letter. This dead letter is used as a weapon in our present history in order to deprive us of our rights in our own land.

Our land has a universal mission

2.3 We believe that our land has a universal mission. In this universality, the meaning of the promises, of the land, of the election, of the people of God open up to include all of humanity, starting from all the peoples of this land. In light of the teachings of the Holy Bible, the promise of the land has never been a political programme, but rather the prelude to complete universal salvation. It was the initiation of the fulfilment of the Kingdom of God on earth.

2.3.1 God sent the patriarchs, the prophets and the apostles to this land so that they might carry forth a universal mission to the world. Today we constitute three religions in this land, Judaism, Christianity and Islam. Our land is God's land, as is the case with all countries in the world. It is holy inasmuch as God is present in it, for God alone is holy and sanctifier. It is the duty of those of us who live here, to respect the will of God for this land. It is our duty to liberate it from the evil of injustice and war. It is God's land and therefore it must be a land of reconciliation, peace and love. This is indeed possible. God has put us here as two peoples, and God gives us the capacity, if we have the will, to live together and establish in it justice and peace, making it in reality God's land: *"The earth is the Lord's and all that is in it, the world, and those who live in it"* (Ps. 24:1).

2.3.2 Our presence in this land, as Christian and Muslim Palestinians, is not accidental but rather deeply rooted in the history and geography of this land, resonant with the connectedness of any other people to the land it lives in. It was an injustice when we were driven out. The West sought to make amends for what Jews had endured in the countries of Europe, but it made amends on our account and in our land. They tried to correct an injustice and the result was a new injustice.

2.3.3 Furthermore, we know that certain theologians in the West try to attach a biblical and theological legitimacy to the infringement of our rights. Thus, the promises, according to their interpretation, have become a menace to our very existence. The "good news" in the Gospel itself has become "a harbinger of death" for us. We call on these theologians to deepen their reflection on the Word of God and to rectify their interpretations so that they might see in the Word of God a source of life for all peoples.

2.3.4 Our connectedness to this land is a natural right. It is not an ideological or a theological question only. It is a matter of life and death. There are those who do not agree with us, even defining us as enemies only because we declare that we want to live as free people in our land. We suffer from the occupation of our land because we are Palestinians. And as Christian Palestinians we suffer from the wrong interpretation of some theologians. Faced with this, our task is to safeguard the Word of God as a source of life and not of death, so that "the good news" remains what it is, "good news" for us and for all. In face of those who use the Bible to threaten our existence as Christian and Muslim Palestinians, we renew our faith in God because we know that the word of God can not be the source of our destruction.

2.4 Therefore, we declare that any use of the Bible to legitimize or support political options and positions that are based upon injustice, imposed by one person on another, or by one people on another, transform religion into human ideology and strip the Word of God of its holiness, its universality and truth.

2.5 We also declare that the Israeli occupation of Palestinian land is a sin against God and humanity because it deprives the Palestinians of their basic human rights, bestowed by God. It distorts the image of God in the Israeli who has become an occupier just as it distorts this image in the Palestinian living under occupation. We declare that any theology, seemingly based on the Bible or on faith or on history, that legitimizes the occupation, is far from Christian teachings, because it calls for violence and holy war in the name of God Almighty, subordinating God to temporary human interests, and distorting the divine image in the human beings living under both political and theological injustice.

3. Hope

3.1 Despite the lack of even a glimmer of positive expectation, our hope remains strong. The present situation does not promise any quick solution or the end of the occupation that is imposed on us. Yes, the initiatives, the conferences, visits and negotiations have multiplied, but they have not been followed up by any change in our situation and suffering. Even the new US position that has been announced by President Obama, with a manifest desire to put an end to the tragedy, has not been able to make a change in our reality. The clear Israeli response, refusing any solution, leaves no room for positive expectation. Despite this, our hope remains strong, because it is from God. God alone is good, almighty and loving and His goodness will one day be victorious over the evil in which we find ourselves. As Saint Paul said: *"If God is for us, who is against us? (...) Who will separate us from the love of Christ? Will hardship, or distress, or persecution, or famine, or nakedness, or peril, or sword? As it is written, "For your sake we are being killed all day long" (...) For I am convinced that (nothing) in all creation, will be able to separate us from the love of God"* (Rom. 8:31, 35, 36, 39).

What is the meaning of hope?

3.2 Hope within us means first and foremost our faith in God and secondly our expectation, despite everything, for a better future. Thirdly, it means not chasing after illusions – we realize that release is not close at hand. Hope is the capacity to see God in the midst of trouble, and to be co-workers with the Holy Spirit who is dwelling in us. From this vision derives the strength to be steadfast, remain firm and work to change the reality in which we find ourselves. Hope means not giving in to evil but rather standing up to it and continuing to resist it. We see nothing in the present or future except ruin and destruction. We see the upper hand of the strong, the growing orientation towards racist separation and the imposition of laws that deny our existence and our dignity. We see confusion and division in the Palestinian position. If, despite all this, we do resist this reality today and work hard, perhaps the destruction that looms on the horizon may not come upon us.

Signs of hope

3.3 The Church in our land, her leaders and her faithful, despite her weakness and her divisions, does show certain signs of hope. Our parish communities are vibrant and most of our young people are active apostles for justice and peace. In addition to the individual commitment, our various Church institutions make our faith active and present in service, love and prayer.

3.3.1 Among the signs of hope are the local centres of theology, with a religious and social character. They are numerous in our different Churches. The ecumenical spirit, even if still hesitant, shows itself more and more in the meetings of our different Church families.

3.3.2 We can add to this the numerous meetings for inter-religious dialogue, Christian–Muslim dialogue, which includes the religious leaders and a part of the people. Admittedly, dialogue is a long process and is perfected through a daily effort as we undergo the same sufferings and have the same expectations. There is also dialogue among the three religions, Judaism, Christianity and Islam, as well as different dialogue meetings on the academic or social level. They all try to breach the walls imposed by the occupation and oppose the distorted perception of human beings in the heart of their brothers or sisters.

3.3.3 One of the most important signs of hope is the steadfastness of the generations, the belief in the justice of their cause and the continuity of memory, which does not forget the "Nakba" (catastrophe) and its significance. Likewise significant is the developing awareness among many Churches throughout the world and their desire to know the truth about what is going on here.

3.3.4 In addition to that, we see a determination among many to overcome the resentments of the past and to be ready for reconciliation once justice has been restored. Public awareness of the need to restore political rights to the Palestinians is increasing, and Jewish and Israeli voices, advocating peace and justice, are raised in support of this with the approval of the international community. True, these forces for justice and reconciliation have not yet been able to transform the situation of injustice, but they have their influence and may shorten the time of suffering and hasten the time of reconciliation.

The mission of the Church

3.4 Our Church is a Church of people who pray and serve. This prayer and service is prophetic, bearing the voice of God in the present and future. Everything that happens in our land, everyone who lives there, all the pains and hopes, all the injustice and all the efforts to stop this injustice, are part and parcel of the prayer of our Church and the service of all her institutions. Thanks be to God that our Church raises her voice against injustice despite the fact that some desire her to remain silent, closed in her religious devotions.

3.4.1 The mission of the Church is prophetic, to speak the Word of God courageously, honestly and lovingly in the local context and in the midst of daily events. If she does take sides, it is with the oppressed, to stand alongside them, just as Christ our Lord stood by the side of each poor person and each sinner, calling them to repentance, life, and the restoration of the dignity bestowed on them by God and that no one has the right to strip away.

3.4.2 The mission of the Church is to proclaim the Kingdom of God, a kingdom of justice, peace and dignity. Our vocation as a living Church is to bear witness to the goodness of God and the dignity of human beings. We are called to pray and to make our voice heard when we announce a new society where human beings believe in their own dignity and the dignity of their adversaries.

3.4.3 Our Church points to the Kingdom, which cannot be tied to any earthly kingdom. Jesus said before Pilate that he was indeed a king but *"my kingdom is not from this world"* (Jn 18:36). Saint Paul says: *"The Kingdom of God is not food and drink but righteousness and peace and joy in the Holy Spirit"* (Rom.14:17). Therefore, religion cannot favour or support any unjust political regime, but must rather promote justice, truth and human dignity. It must exert every effort to purify regimes where human beings suffer injustice and human dignity is violated. The Kingdom of God on earth is not dependent on any political orientation, for it is greater and more inclusive than any particular political system.

3.4.4 Jesus Christ said: *"The Kingdom of God is among you"* (Luke 17:21). This Kingdom that is present among us and in us is the extension of the mystery of salvation. It is the presence of God among us and our sense of that presence in everything we do and say. It is in this divine presence that we shall do what we can until justice is achieved in this land .

3.4.5 The cruel circumstances in which the Palestinian Church has lived and continues to live have required the Church to clarify her faith and to identify her vocation better. We have studied our vocation and have come to know it better in the midst of suffering and pain: today, we bear the strength of love rather than that of revenge, a culture of life rather than a culture of death. This is a source of hope for us, for the Church and for the world.

3.5 The Resurrection is the source of our hope .Just as Christ rose in victory over death and evil, so too we are able, as each inhabitant of this land is able, to vanquish the evil of war. We will remain a witnessing, steadfast and active Church in the land of the Resurrection.

4. Love

The commandment of love

4.1 Christ our Lord said: *"Just as I have loved you, you also should love one another"* (Jn 13:34). He has already showed us how to love and how to treat our enemies. He said: *"You have heard that it was said, 'You shall love your neighbour and hate your enemy.' But I say to you, Love your enemies and pray for those who persecute you, so that you may be children of your Father in heaven; for he makes his sun rise on the evil and on the good, and sends rain on the righteous and on the unrighteous (...) Be perfect, therefore, as your heavenly Father is perfect"* (Matt. 5:45-47). Saint Paul also said: *"Do not repay anyone evil for evil"* (Rom. 12:17). And Saint Peter said: *"Do not repay evil for evil or abuse for abuse; but on the contrary, repay with a blessing. It is for this that you were called"* (1 Pet. 3:9).

Resistance

4.2 This word is clear. Love is the commandment of Christ our Lord to us and it includes both friends and enemies. This must be clear when we find ourselves in circumstances where we must resist evil of whatever kind.

4.2.1 Love is seeing the face of God in every human being. Every person is my brother or my sister. However, seeing the face of God in everyone does not mean accepting evil or aggression on their part. Rather, this love seeks to correct the evil and stop the aggression. The aggression against the Palestinian people which is the Israeli occupation, is an evil that must be resisted. It is an evil and a sin that must be resisted and removed. Primary responsibility for this rests with the Palestinians themselves suffering occupation. Christian love invites us to resist it. However, love puts an end to evil by walking in the ways of justice. Responsibility lies also with the international community, because international law regulates relations between peoples today. Finally responsibility lies with the perpetrators of the injustice; they must liberate themselves from the evil that is in them and the injustice they have imposed on others.

4.2.2 When we review the history of the nations, we see many wars and much resistance to war by war, to violence by violence. The Palestinian people has gone the way of the peoples, particularly in the first stages of its struggle with the Israeli occupation. However, it also engaged in peaceful struggle, especially during the first Intifada. We recognize that all peoples must find a new way in their relations with each other and the resolution of their conflicts. The ways of force must give way to the ways of justice. This applies above all to the peoples that are militarily strong, mighty enough to impose their injustice on the weaker.

4.2.3 We say that our option as Christians in the face of the Israeli occupation is to resist. Resistance is a right and a duty for the Christian. But it is resistance with love as its logic. It is thus a creative resistance for it must find human ways that engage the humanity of the enemy. Seeing the image of God in the face of the enemy means taking up positions in the light of this vision of active resistance to stop the injustice and oblige the perpetrator to end his aggression and thus achieve the desired goal, which is getting back the land, freedom, dignity and independence.

4.2.4 Christ our Lord has left us an example we must imitate. We must resist evil but he taught us that we cannot resist evil with evil. This is a difficult commandment, particularly when the enemy is determined to impose himself and deny our right to remain here in our land. It is a difficult commandment yet it alone can stand firm in the face of the clear declarations of the occupation authorities that refuse our existence and the many excuses these authorities use to continue imposing occupation upon us.

4.2.5 Resistance to the evil of occupation is integrated, then, within this Christian love that refuses evil and corrects it. It resists evil in all its forms with methods that enter into the logic of love and draw on all energies to make peace. We can resist through civil disobedience. We do not resist with death but rather through respect of life. We respect and have a high esteem for all those who have given their life for our nation. And we affirm that every citizen must be ready to defend his or her life, freedom and land.

4.2.6 Palestinian civil organizations, as well as international organizations, NGOs and certain religious institutions call on individuals, companies and states to engage in divestment and in an economic and commercial boycott of everything produced by the occupation. We understand this to integrate the logic of peaceful resistance.

These advocacy campaigns must be carried out with courage, openly sincerely proclaiming that their object is not revenge but rather to put an end to the existing evil, liberating both the perpetrators and the victims of injustice. The aim is to free both peoples from extremist positions of the different Israeli governments, bringing both to justice and reconciliation. In this spirit and with this dedication we will eventually reach the longed-for resolution to our problems, as indeed happened in South Africa and with many other liberation movements in the world.

4.3 Through our love, we will overcome injustices and establish foundations for a new society both for us and for our opponents. Our future and their future are one. Either the cycle of violence that destroys both of us or peace that will benefit both. We call on Israel to give up its injustice towards us, not to twist the truth of reality of the occupation by pretending that it is a battle against terrorism. The roots of "terrorism" are in the human injustice committed and in the evil of the occupation. These must be removed if there be a sincere intention to remove "terrorism". We call on the people of Israel to be our partners in peace and not in the cycle of interminable violence. Let us resist evil together, the evil of occupation and the infernal cycle of violence.

5. Our word to our brothers and sisters

5.1 We all face, today, a way that is blocked and a future that promises only woe. Our word to all our Christian brothers and sisters is a word of hope, patience, steadfastness and new action for a better future. Our word is that we, as Christians we carry a message, and we will continue to carry it despite the thorns, despite blood and daily difficulties. We place our hope in God, who will grant us relief in His own time. At the same time, we continue to act in concord with God and God's will, building, resisting evil and bringing closer the day of justice and peace.

5.2 We say to our Christian brothers and sisters: This is a time for repentance. Repentance brings us back into the communion of love with everyone who suffers, the prisoners, the wounded, those afflicted with temporary or permanent handicaps, the children who cannot live their childhood and each one who mourns a dear one. The communion of love says to every believer in spirit and in truth: if my brother is a prisoner I am a prisoner; if his home is destroyed, my home is destroyed; when my brother is killed, then I too am killed. We face the same challenges and share in all that has happened and will happen. Perhaps, as individuals or as heads of Churches, we were silent when we should have raised our voices to condemn the injustice and share in the suffering. This is a time of repentance for our silence, indifference, lack of communion, either because we did not persevere in our mission in this land and abandoned it, or because we did not think and do enough to reach a new and integrated vision and remained divided, contradicting our witness and weakening our word. Repentance for our concern with our institutions, sometimes at the expense of our mission, thus silencing the prophetic voice given by the Spirit to the Churches.

5.3 We call on Christians to remain steadfast in this time of trial, just as we have throughout the centuries, through the changing succession of states and governments. Be patient, steadfast and full of hope so that you might fill the heart of every one of your brothers or sisters who shares in this same trial with hope. *"Always be ready to make your defence to anyone who demands from you an accounting for the hope that is in you"* (1 Pet. 3:15). Be active and, provided this conforms to love, participate in any sacrifice that resistance asks of you to overcome our present travail ..

5.4 Our numbers are few but our message is great and important. Our land is in urgent need of love. Our love is a message to the Muslim and to the Jew, as well as to the world.

5.4.1 Our message to the Muslims is a message of love and of living together and a call to reject fanaticism and extremism. It is also a message to the world that Muslims are neither to be stereotyped as the enemy nor caricatured as terrorists but rather to be lived with in peace and engaged with in dialogue.

5.4.2 Our message to the Jews tells them: Even though we have fought one another in the recent past and still struggle today, we are able to love and live together. We can organize our political life, with all its complexity, according to the logic of this love and its power, after ending the occupation and establishing justice.

5.4.3 The word of faith says to anyone engaged in political activity: human beings were not made for hatred. It is not permitted to hate, neither is it permitted to kill or to be killed. The culture of love is the culture of accepting the other. Through it we perfect ourselves and the foundations of society are established.

6. Our word to the Churches of the world

6.1 Our word to the Churches of the world is firstly a word of gratitude for the solidarity you have shown toward us in word, deed and presence among us. It is a word of praise for the many Churches and Christians who support the right of the Palestinian people for self determination. It is a message of solidarity with those Christians and Churches who have suffered because of their advocacy for law and justice . However, it is also a call to repentance; to revisit fundamentalist theological positions that support certain unjust political options with regard to the Palestinian people. It is a call to stand alongside the oppressed and preserve the word of God as good news for all rather than to turn it into a weapon with which to slay the oppressed. The word of God is a word of love for all His creation. God is not the ally of one against the other, nor the opponent of one in the face of the other. God is the Lord of all and loves all, demanding justice from all and issuing to all of us the same commandments. We ask our sister Churches not to offer a theological cover-up for the injustice we suffer, for the sin of the occupation imposed upon us. Our question to our brothers and sisters in the Churches today is: Are you able to help us get our freedom back, for this is the only way you can help the two peoples attain justice, peace, security and love?

6.2 In order to understand our reality, we say to the Churches: Come and see. We will fulfil our role to make known to you the truth of our reality, receiving you as pilgrims coming to us to pray, carrying a message of peace, love and reconciliation. You will know the facts and the people of this land, Palestinians and Israelis alike.

6.3 We condemn all forms of racism, whether religious or ethnic, including anti-Semitism and Islamophobia, and we call on you to condemn it and oppose it in all its manifestations. At the same time we call on you to say a word of truth and to take a position of truth with regard to Israel's occupation of Palestinian land. As we have already said, we see boycott and disinvestment as tools of non violence for justice, peace and security for all.

7. Our word to the international community

7. Our word to the international community is to stop the principle of "double standards" and insist on the international resolutions regarding the Palestinian problem with regard to all parties. Selective application of international law threatens to leave us vulnerable to a law of the jungle. It legitimizes the claims by certain armed groups and states that the international community only understands the logic of force. Therefore, we call for a response to what the civil and religious institutions have proposed, as mentioned earlier: the beginning of a system of economic sanctions and boycott to

be applied against Israel. We repeat once again that this is not revenge but rather a serious action in order to reach a just and definitive peace that will put an end to Israeli occupation of Palestinian and other Arab territories and will guarantee security and peace for all.

8. Jewish and Muslim religious leaders

8. Finally, we address an appeal to the religious and spiritual leaders, Jewish and Muslim, with whom we share the same vision that every human being is created by God and has been given equal dignity. Hence the obligation for each of us to defend the oppressed and the dignity God has bestowed on them. Let us together try to rise up above the political positions that have failed so far and continue to lead us on the path of failure and suffering.

9. A call to our Palestinian people and to the Israelis

9.1 This is a call to see the face of God in each one of God's creatures and overcome the barriers of fear or race in order to establish a constructive dialogue and not remain within the cycle of never-ending manoeuvres that aim to keep the situation as it is. Our appeal is to reach a common vision, built on equality and sharing, not on superiority, negation of the other or aggression, using the pretext of fear and security. We say that love is possible and mutual trust is possible. Thus, peace is possible and definitive reconciliation also. Thus, justice and security will be attained for all.

9.2 Education is important. Educational programs must help us to get to know the other as he or she is rather than through the prism of conflict, hostility or religious fanaticism. The educational programs in place today are infected with this hostility. The time has come to begin a new education that allows one to see the face of God in the other and declares that we are capable of loving each other and building our future together in peace and security.

9.3 Trying to make the state a religious state, Jewish or Islamic, suffocates the state, confines it within narrow limits, and transforms it into a state that practices discrimination and exclusion, preferring one citizen over another. We appeal to both religious Jews and Muslims: let the state be a state for all its citizens, with a vision constructed on respect for religion but also equality, justice, liberty and respect for pluralism and not on domination by a religion or a numerical majority.

9.4 To the leaders of Palestine we say that current divisions weaken all of us and cause more sufferings. Nothing can justify these divisions. For the good of the people, which must outweigh that of the political parties, an end must be put to division. We appeal to the international community to lend its support towards this union and to respect the will of the Palestinian people as expressed freely.

9.5 Jerusalem is the foundation of our vision and our entire life. She is the city to which God gave a particular importance in the history of humanity. She is the city towards which all people are in movement – and where they will meet in friendship and love in the presence of the One Unique God, according to the vision of the prophet Isaiah: *"In days to come the mountain of the Lord's house shall be established as the highest of the mountains, and shall be raised above the hills; all the nations shall stream to it (...) He shall judge between the nations, and shall arbitrate for many peoples; they shall beat their swords into ploughshares, and their spears into pruning hooks; nation shall not lift up sword against nation, neither shall they learn war any more"* (Is. 2:2-5). Today, the city is inhabited by two peoples of three religions; and it is on this prophetic vision and on the international resolutions concerning the totality of Jerusalem that any political solution must be based. This is the first issue that should be negotiated because the recognition of Jerusalem's sanctity and its message will be a source of inspiration towards finding a solution to the entire problem, which is largely a problem of mutual trust and ability to set in place a new land in this land of God.

10. Hope and faith in God

10. In the absence of all hope, we cry out our cry of hope. We believe in God, good and just. We believe that God's goodness will finally triumph over the evil of hate and of death that still persist in our land. We will see here "a new land" and "a new human being", capable of rising up in the spirit to love each one of his or her brothers and sisters.

A Message from the Authors

This document is the Christian Palestinians' word to the world about what is happening in Palestine. It is written at this time when we wanted to see the Glory of the grace of God in this land and in the sufferings of its people. In this spirit the document requests the international community to stand by the Palestinian people who have faced oppression, displacement, suffering and clear apartheid for more than six decades. The suffering continues while the international community silently looks on at the occupying State, Israel. Our word is a cry of hope, with love, prayer and faith in God. We address it first of all to ourselves and then to all the churches and Christians in the world, asking them to stand against injustice and apartheid, urging them to work for a just peace in our region, calling on them to revisit theologies that justify crimes perpetrated against our people and the dispossession of the land.

In this historic document, we Palestinian Christians declare that the military occupation of our land is a sin against God and humanity, and that any theology that legitimizes the occupation is far from Christian teachings because true Christian theology is a theology of love and solidarity with the oppressed, a call to justice and equality among peoples. This document did not come about spontaneously, and it is not the result of a coincidence. It is not a theoretical theological study or a policy paper, but is rather a document of faith and work. Its importance stems from the sincere expression of the concerns of the people and their view of this moment in history we are living through. It seeks to be prophetic in addressing things as they are without equivocation and with boldness, in addition it puts forward ending the Israeli occupation of Palestinian land and all forms of discrimination as the solution that will lead to a just and lasting peace with the establishment of an independent Palestinian state with Al-Quds as its capital. The document also demands that all peoples, political leaders and decision-makers put pressure on Israel and take legal measures in order to oblige its government to put an end to its oppression and disregard for the international law. The document also holds a clear position that non-violent resistance to this injustice is a right and duty for all Palestinians including Christians.

The initiators of this document have been working on it for more than a year, in prayer and discussion, guided by their faith in God and their love for their people, accepting advice from many friends: Palestinians, Arabs and those from the wider international community. We are grateful to our friends for their solidarity with us. As Palestinian Christians we hope that this document will provide the turning point to focus the efforts of all peace-loving peoples in the world, especially our Christian sisters and brothers. We hope also that it will be welcomed positively and will receive strong support, as was the South Africa Kairos document launched in 1985, which, at that time proved to be a tool in the struggle against oppression and occupation. We believe that liberation from occupation is in the interest of all peoples in the region because the problem is not just a political one, but one in which human beings are destroyed. We pray God to inspire us all, particularly our leaders and policy-makers, to find the way of justice and equality, and to realize that it is the only way that leads to the genuine peace we are seeking.

With thanks,

- His Beatitude Patriarch Michel Sabbah
- His Grace Bishop Dr. Munib Younan
- His Eminence Archbishop Atallah Hanna
- Rev. Dr. Jamal Khader
- Rev. Dr. Rafiq Khoury
- Rev. Dr. Mitri Raheb
- Rev. Dr. Naim Ateek
- Rev. Dr. Yohana Katanacho

- Rev. Fadi Diab
- Dr. Jiries Khoury
- Ms. Cedar Duaybis
- Ms. Nora Kort
- Ms. Lucy Thaljieh
- Mr. Nidal Abu El Zuluf
- Mr. Yusef Daher
- Mr. Rifat Kassis - Coordinator

We hear the cry of our children

We, the Patriarchs and Heads of Churches in Jerusalem, hear the cry of hope that our children have launched in these difficult times that we still experience in this Holy Land. We support them and stand by them in their faith, their hope, their love and their vision for the future. We also support the call to all our faithful as well as to the Israeli and Palestinian Leaders, to the International Community and to the World Churches, in order to accelerate the achievement of justice, peace and reconciliation in this Holy Land. We ask God to bless all our children by giving them more power in order to contribute effectively in establishing and developing their community, while making it a community in love, trust, justice and peace.

- His Beatitude Theophilos III, Greek Orthodox
- His Beatitude Patriarch Fouad Twal, Latin Church
- His Beatitude Patriarch Torkom Manougian, Armenian Orthodox
- Very Revd Father Pierbattista Pizzaballa, Custody of the Holy Land
- H.E. Archbishop Dr Anba Abraham, Coptic
- H.E. Archbishop Mar Swerios Malki Murad, Syrian Orthodox
- H.E. Archbishop Paul Nabil Sayah, Maronite

- H.E. Archbishop Abba Mathaious, Ethiopian
- H.E. Archbishop Joseph-Jules Zerey, Greek Catholic
- Bishop Gregor Peter Malki, Syrian Catholic
- Bishop Munib A. Younan, Lutheran
- Bishop Suheil Dawani, Anglican
- Bishop Raphael Minassian, Armenian Catholic

December 15, 2009

Note: A list of Palestinian Christian institutions and personalities that have signed the *Kairos Palestine* document and copies of the document in other languages are available at www.kairospalestine.ps

Photo: CPT Palestine

Christian Peacemaker Teams have been working in Hebron since 1998. Here, team members accompany kindergarten children home from school. *Read more about CPT on page 15.*

www.ingramcontent.com/pod-product-compliance
Lightning Source LLC
Chambersburg PA
CBHW080554030426
42337CB00024B/4870